THE ULTIMATE

Chameleon

BOOK FOR KIDS

JENNY KELLETT

CONTENTS

MEET THE CHAMELEONS

Have you ever wondered how the incredible chameleon changes its colors? Or maybe you're curious about where these extraordinary creatures hang out when they're not busy being the superheroes of the animal kingdom? Well, you've just opened the perfect book to discover all these jaw-dropping, eye-popping facts about chameleons—and much more!

In *The Ultimate Chameleon Book for Kids*, we're going on an epic adventure to explore the wondrous world of these color-changing critters.

From the tropical forests of Madagascar to the sandy deserts of Africa, chameleons are here, there, and everywhere! And guess what? You don't need to pack your bags or even leave your cozy reading nook, because this book is your VIP ticket to Chameleon Land.

A group of chameleons is called a clan. However, chameleons prefer to be alone!

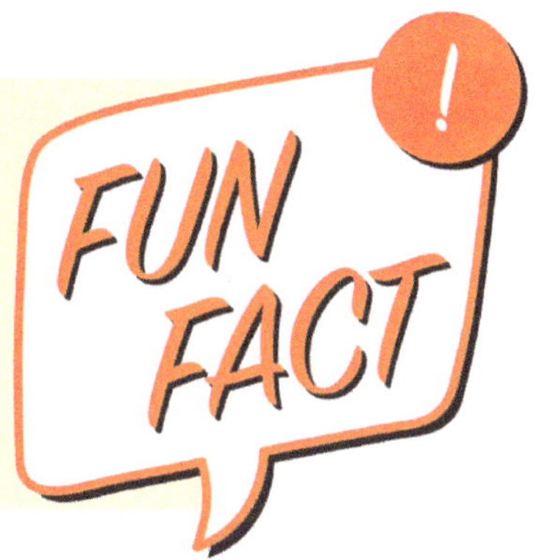

HERE'S A SNEAK-PEEK OF THE AWESOMENESS COMING YOUR WAY:

⭐ Ever heard of a panther chameleon? How about a veiled chameleon? Get ready to meet these fellas and more!

⭐ Discover how chameleons use their one-of-a-kind vision to scan their surroundings like real-life spies!

⭐ Learn how these camouflage experts change their colors to express their feelings. Yup, they're the original mood rings!

⭐ Want to become a chameleon hero? Learn how you can help chameleons be their best selves in the wild.

⭐ And guess what? We've got quizzes, fun facts, and unbelievable stories that will make you the go-to chameleon guru among your friends!

So are you ready to learn more about chameleons? We are!

LET'S DO THIS!

WHAT ARE CHAMELEONS?

Chameleons are a kind of lizard, but they're not your ordinary, run-of-the-mill reptiles. These creatures belong to the family called Chamaeleonidae, which sounds like a name right out of a wizarding book, doesn't it? Unlike most lizards, chameleons have some very unique features, such as their zig-zagging walk, incredibly long tongues, and of course, their ability to change color.

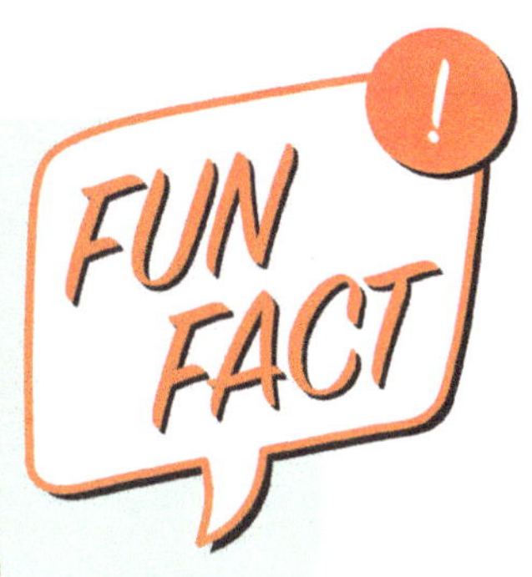

The name "chameleon" comes from a Greek word 'khamai,' which means "on the ground," and 'leon,' which means "lion." Imagine that—a ground lion that can change colors!

WHERE DO CHAMELEONS LIVE?

If you're on a quest to find a chameleon, you might have to travel pretty far. These little adventurers are mostly found in warm climates. Places like Madagascar, Africa, southern Europe, and even some parts of Asia are where they call home. Each area has its own unique species adapted to that particular environment.

Madagascar is like the ultimate chameleon playground! More than half of the world's chameleon species can be found there.

A VARIETY OF SPECIES

When we say chameleons come in all shapes and sizes, we really mean it. There are around 160 species of chameleons, and each has its own unique look and style. Some are as tiny as your finger, while others can grow as long as a foot. Some like to climb trees; others prefer to stick closer to the ground.

DID YOU KNOW?!

The world's smallest chameleon is the Brookesia micra**, and it can fit on a matchstick!**

WHAT MAKES THEM SO UNIQUE?

If the chameleon was a student in a classroom, it would be the kid with all the coolest gadgets and tricks up their sleeves. One of the most fascinating features of a chameleon is its tongue. These creatures have a tongue that can be up to 1.5 times the length of their body! They use it to catch insects by shooting it out at incredible speed.

DID YOU KNOW?!

A chameleon's tongue can accelerate more than 41 g, which is over 400 times the force of gravity. That's faster than a fighter jet taking off!

MORE THAN JUST COLOR CHANGERS

Many people know chameleons for their color-changing abilities, but there's so much more to these creatures than meets the eye—literally! Their eyes can move independently of each other, allowing them to look in two different directions at the same time. This is a huge advantage when they're on the hunt or trying to avoid predators.

DID YOU KNOW?!

Chameleons have a full 360-degree view around their body. Talk about having eyes in the back of your head!

Did you know that there are around 160 different species of chameleons in the world? That's right! These fascinating reptiles come in all sorts of shapes, sizes, and colors, each with their own unique abilities and styles.

In this chapter, let's get to know some of the standout members of this extraordinary family.

VEILED CHAMELEON

(Scientific name: *Chamaeleo calyptratus*)

WHERE THEY LIVE: The veiled chameleon, also called the Yemen chameleon, is a native of Saudi Arabia and Yemen.

CHARACTERISTICS: One of the most noticeable features of the veiled chameleon is its casque, a helmet-like ridge on its head. This species often has stunning bands of gold, green, and blue along its body, making it a favorite among pet owners.

FUN FACT: The casque on a veiled chameleon's head isn't just for show; it helps to direct water towards their mouth.

PANTHER CHAMELEON

(Scientific name: *Furcifer pardalis*)

WHERE THEY LIVE: The native home of the panther chameleon is Madagascar.

CHARACTERISTICS: These chameleons come in a spectacular range of colors depending on their geographic location.

FUN FACT: Male panther chameleons are more colorful than their female counterparts. They change colors according to their mood and to attract mates. They literally wear their emotions on their scales!

JACKSON'S CHAMELEON

(Scientific name: *Trioceros jacksonii*)

WHERE THEY LIVE: They call East Africa home.

CHARACTERISTICS: This species is famous for its three horns and a more muted color palette than other chameleons.

FUN FACT: Those horns are not just for decoration; they're mainly used to impress females during the mating season. A real Casanova, this one!

SENEGAL CHAMELEON
(Scientific name: *Chamaeleo senegalensis*)

WHERE THEY LIVE: This adaptable chameleon prefers the varied landscapes of West Africa, from forests to savannas.

CHARACTERISTICS: With a simpler color palette ranging from green to brown, this chameleon is one of the most adaptable species out there.

FUN FACT: Senegal chameleons are often found in pairs and have a unique dance they perform when meeting another chameleon. Think of it as their own secret handshake!

© Farid Amadou Bahleman

FLAP-NECKED CHAMELEON

(Scientific name: *Chamaeleo dilepis*)

WHERE THEY LIVE: The flap-necked chameleon is a native of Sub-Saharan Africa, where it lives in a range of habitats.

CHARACTERISTICS: This species gets its name from the flaps of skin that frame either side of its neck.

FUN FACT: You might think those flaps are just for show, but they serve an essential function! When the chameleon feels threatened, it can extend these neck flaps to appear larger and more intimidating to predators.

OUSTALET'S CHAMELEON

(Scientific name: *Furcifer oustaleti*)

WHERE THEY LIVE: This species primarily resides in Madagascar, but it has also been found in parts of East Africa.

CHARACTERISTICS: It is one of the largest chameleons, capable of reaching lengths of up to 30 inches. Its coloration is often a mix of browns and greens.

FUN FACT: Due to its size, the Oustalet's chameleon has a different diet from smaller chameleons. They have been known to eat small birds and rodents, not just insects!

© Charles J. Sharp

PARSON'S CHAMELEON

(Scientific name: *Calumma parsonii*)

WHERE THEY LIVE: This reclusive chameleon is native to the rainforests of Madagascar.

CHARACTERISTICS: The Parson's chameleon is one of the largest and heaviest chameleons, and it has a life span that can exceed a decade. Its colors can vary widely, from shades of green and blue to orange and yellow.

FUN FACT: Unlike many chameleons that have shorter lifespans, the Parson's chameleon can live for up to 20 years in captivity!

© JialiangGao

WHAT DO THEY HAVE IN COMMON?

All chameleons share some cool features, like **zygodactyl** feet for climbing, super-long tongues for snatching up meals, and eyes that move independently of each other.

FUN FACT

Did you know that all chameleons are excellent climbers?
They even have a **prehensile** tail that acts like a fifth hand to help them grip branches tightly.

CHAMELEON ANATOMY 101

WELCOME TO THE MOST EXCITING ANATOMY CLASS YOU'LL EVER ATTEND!

If chameleons were superheroes, this chapter would be about their superpowers. From their color-changing skin to their ultra-long tongues and rotating eyes, each body part serves a unique purpose, making chameleons some of the most extraordinary creatures on the planet. So let's dissect (not literally!) the marvels of chameleon anatomy.

While many animals have unique features, chameleons take it to the next level. They've got specialized cells called chromatophores that allow them to change color. More on that soon!

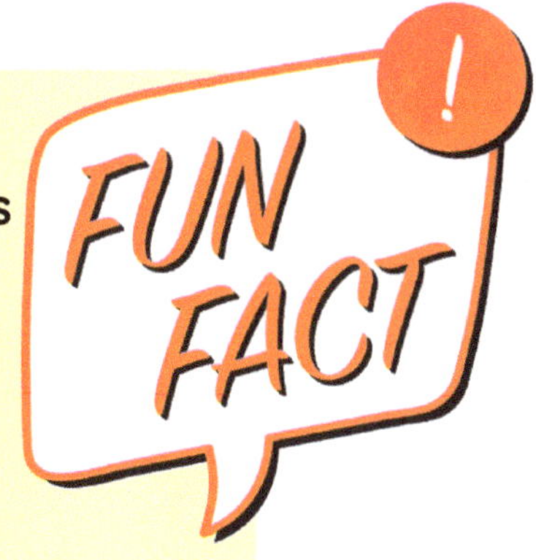

THE TONGUE
A BUILT-IN FISHING ROD

Let's start with one of the chameleon's most iconic features: its tongue. Imagine having a fishing rod that could shoot out from your mouth—that's what a chameleon has! Its tongue can be up to 1.5 times the length of its body and can shoot out in just 0.07 seconds to catch insects. The sticky tip ensures that their prey has no chance of escape.

A chameleon's tongue is coiled inside its mouth like a spring. When it's time to strike, the muscles uncoil rapidly, propelling the tongue forward at lightning speed!

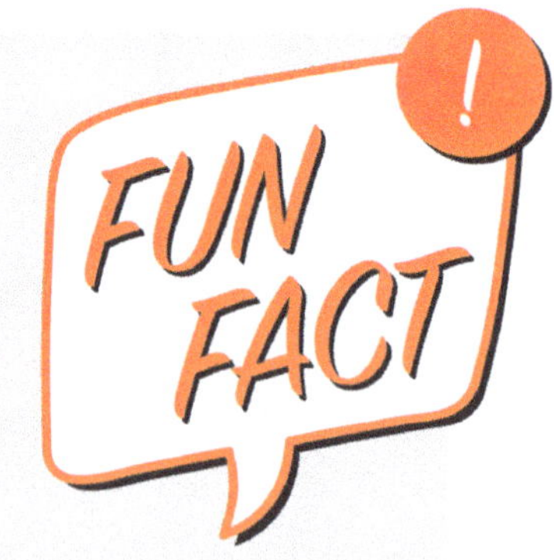

THE EYES
360-DEGREE VISION

Wouldn't it be awesome to have eyes in the back of your head? Chameleons pretty much do! Their eyes can move independently, giving them a full 360-degree view of their surroundings. This is incredibly useful for spotting both prey and predators. And get this—they can zoom in and out for a closer look, just like a camera lens!

 **FUN FACT:** Chameleons have excellent eyesight for their size. They can even see in both visible and ultraviolet light, allowing them to perceive their world in a way humans can't.

THE SKIN
THE ORIGINAL MOOD RING

The ability to change color is perhaps the most fascinating feature of a chameleon. But they don't just do it for camouflage. Their skin can also reflect their mood, temperature, and even intentions toward other chameleons. Layers of specialized cells, known as **chromatophores**, control this ability. Each layer contains different pigments that can expand or contract to produce a stunning array of colors.

Chameleons can't produce every color. They can't turn red, for instance, unless they have red pigments in their skin cells. So, they're somewhat limited by their natural color palette.

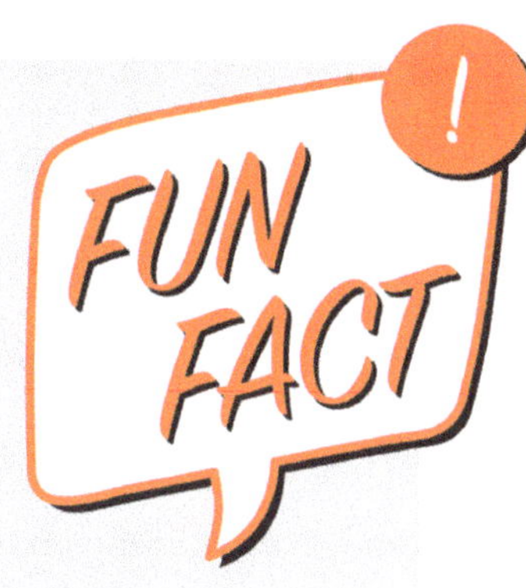

A Fischer chameleon.

THE FEET AND TAIL: CLIMBING TOOLS

Last but not least, let's talk about their feet and tail. Chameleons have **zygodactyl** feet—two toes facing forward and two facing backward—that provide an excellent grip for climbing. Their prehensile tail is another vital tool, acting like a fifth limb that helps them balance and navigate through trees and shrubs.

A chameleon's tail is so strong and flexible, it can support the animal's entire body weight for a short period. This comes in handy when they need an extra "hand" to grab onto branches.

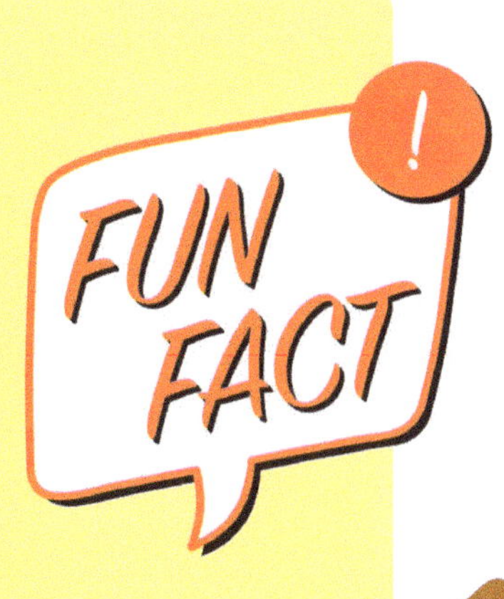

WHAT'S FOR DINNER?

If chameleons had a cooking show, it wouldn't just feature fast food; it would be a masterclass in the art of quick capture. What's on the menu for these remarkable reptiles? Let's dig into the fascinating world of chameleon diets.

Dining in the Wild: The Bug Buffet

The majority of chameleons are **insectivores**, meaning they primarily eat insects. Crickets, locusts, and even spiders are some of the items on their wild menu. For chameleons living in rainforests, the selection can include more exotic dishes like mantises and stick insects.

The veiled chameleon has been known to eat plants and leaves in addition to insects. They're like the flexitarians of the chameleon world!

FUN FACT

Chameleons can
eat up to 50 insects
a day when food is
plentiful.

Special Dietary Needs: Picky Eaters? Not So Much!

Chameleons aren't too fussy when it comes to food, but they do have some dietary requirements to keep them healthy. For instance, they need calcium for strong bones (yes, chameleons worry about their health too!). In the wild, they often consume insects that have eaten plants rich in nutrients, covering their dietary bases without even knowing it.

⭐ **FUN FACT:** **Captive chameleons often require vitamin and calcium supplements to keep them healthy, especially if they're not exposed to natural sunlight.**

FEEDING TACTICS: AIM, SHOOT, FEAST!

The chameleon's long, sticky tongue is its primary tool for catching prey. It can extend in the blink of an eye, adhering to whatever unlucky insect happens to be in its path. But they also use their incredible eyesight to spot potential meals from a distance, essentially aiming before they shoot their tongues out.

A chameleon's tongue has a special muscle structure that makes it incredibly flexible and accurate, ensuring they rarely miss a meal.

Chameleons don't have good depth perception when it comes to still water. That's why they prefer to drink moving water, like raindrops or dew.

DO CHAMELEONS DRINK WATER?

You may already be wondering how chameleons quench their thirst. They don't have access to water bottles, after all! In the wild, they usually lap up dew and raindrops from leaves. Some species will even use their casque to channel water toward their mouths. Yep, they have built-in water slides!

CHAMELEON
HABITATS

Where in the World Do Chameleons Live?

Picture this: You're a chameleon, and you get to pick your dream home. Would you choose a lush rainforest, a dry desert, or maybe a tropical island?

Good news! Chameleons have such a wide range of habitats that they're almost like world travelers—without the need for passports. Let's zoom in on the atlas and see where these cool creatures hang out and how they adapt to their unique homes.

FUN FACT: While many people think chameleons are only from Madagascar, they actually inhabit multiple continents including Africa, Asia, and even a small part of Europe!

RAINFORESTS: THE ULTIMATE JUNGLE GYM

Rainforests are like five-star resorts for chameleons. With plenty of trees to climb and an all-you-can-eat buffet of insects, it's paradise for tree-loving species. The high humidity also helps them keep their skin moist. Animals like the Parson's chameleon and many species of dwarf chameleons call this leafy wonderland home.

FUN FACT: In the rainforest, chameleons often choose branches that are just the right size for their feet, making it easier for them to grip and climb.

The Deserts: Mastering the Art of Survival

You might be surprised to find chameleons like the Namaqua living in deserts, where conditions can be harsh. They've developed some nifty survival skills, like burrowing into the sand to escape the heat or to catch some z's at night. Their color-changing abilities come in extra handy here, allowing them to reflect light and stay cool.

Some desert chameleons can flatten their bodies to minimize contact with hot sand, keeping themselves cooler. Now, that's innovative!
FUN FACT
!

The Highlands and Mountains: The Sky's the Limit

Yes, there are some chameleons adventurous enough to live in high altitudes. The Jackson's chameleon, for example, is found in the highlands of East Africa. Their thick skin and slow metabolism help them adapt to the cooler temperatures found at lofty heights. Chameleons living at high altitudes tend to have darker coloration. This helps them absorb more sunlight to stay warm.

Coastal and Island Habitats: Living the Island Life

Some chameleons like to feel the sea breeze on their scales. Coastal and island habitats, especially in places like Madagascar, are home to various species, including the Labord's chameleon (above). These environments offer plenty of vegetation and a moderate climate.

Island chameleons often have fewer predators, which has led to some unique behaviors and adaptations not seen in their mainland cousins.

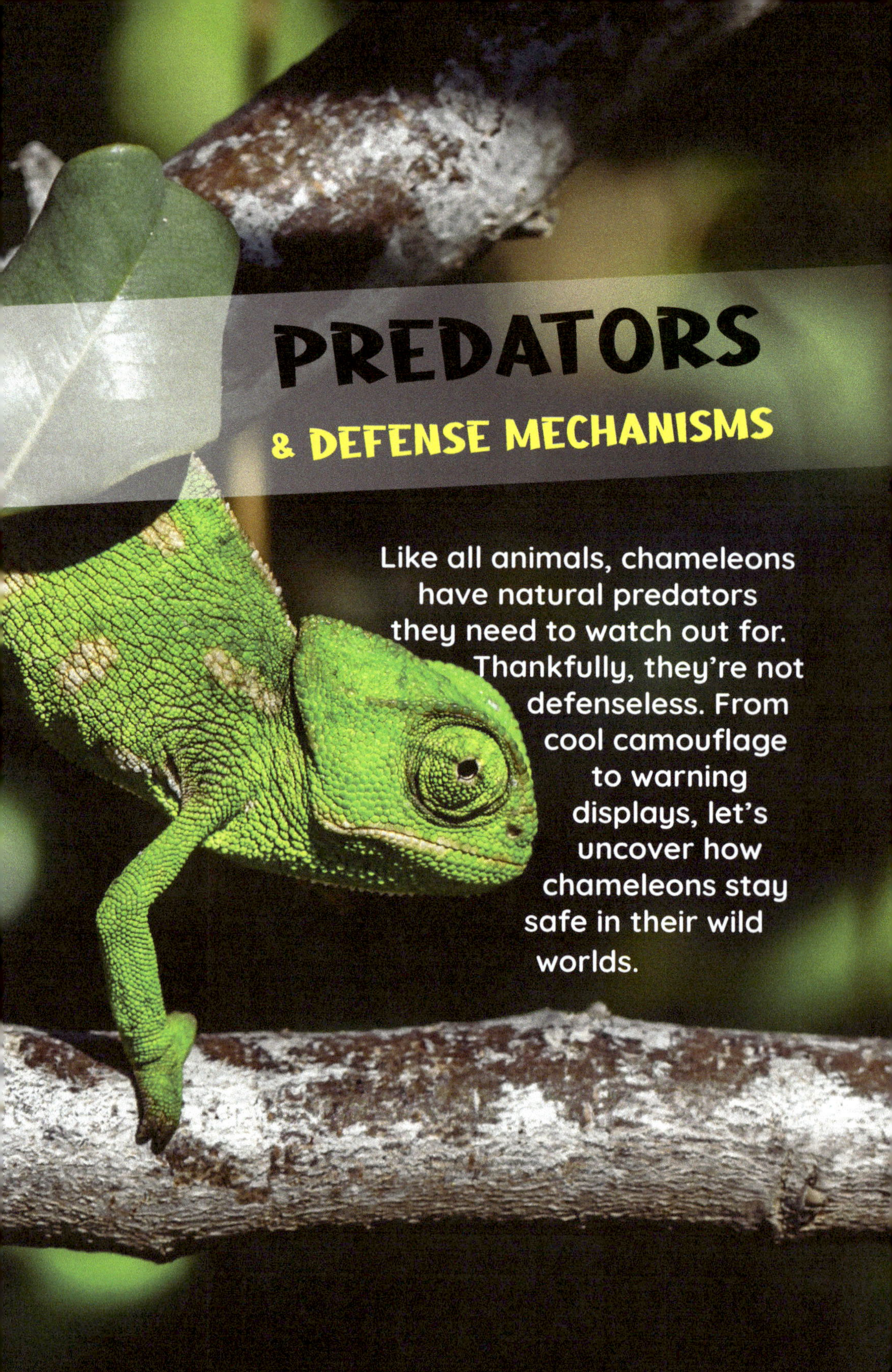

PREDATORS
& DEFENSE MECHANISMS

Like all animals, chameleons have natural predators they need to watch out for. Thankfully, they're not defenseless. From cool camouflage to warning displays, let's uncover how chameleons stay safe in their wild worlds.

Some chameleons can puff up their bodies to appear bigger and more threatening to predators.

WHO'S HUNGRY FOR CHAMELEONS?

In the animal kingdom, it's a tough world out there. Snakes, birds, and even larger lizards often have chameleons on their menu. Baby chameleons are especially vulnerable and have to be extra cautious to avoid becoming a quick snack.

FUN FACT: Predators aren't the only danger for chameleons. They also have to watch out for parasitic insects that can make them sick.

THE ART OF CAMOUFLAGE

One of the chameleon's most famous defense mechanisms is its ability to change color. While this skill is often used for communication and temperature control, it also serves as an effective camouflage. By blending in with their surroundings, chameleons can become nearly invisible to predators. This is especially useful when they're trying to escape or hide.

FUN FACT: Some chameleons have patterns that mimic leaves or branches, making them masters of disguise!

If camouflage fails or if a chameleon decides it's time to stand its ground, many species have unique ways of signaling danger. Some may hiss, puff up their bodies, or even display bright warning colors to scare off potential threats. It's their way of saying, "Back off, buddy!"

FUN FACT:
Panther chameleons (pictured right) can display vibrant colors and patterns to deter predators and signal that they are not to be messed with.

Chameleons usually move slowly to avoid detection, but when danger strikes, they can surprisingly pick up the pace!

FUN FACT

THE QUICK ESCAPE

Chameleons may not win a race against a cheetah, but they're pretty agile when they need to be. Their zygodactyl feet and prehensile tails are not just for climbing; they also assist in making a quick getaway. They can dart between branches and leaves, using their unique anatomy to navigate complex terrains.

THE SCIENCE
BEHIND THE
COLOR CHANGE

For chameleons, changing colors is just another day in their super-cool lives. But why do they do it? Prepare to have your minds blown.

A chameleon's skin has several layers of specialized cells filled with pigments, which allow them to create a spectrum of colors.

HOW DO THEY CHANGE COLOR?

Before we get into the "why," let's talk about the "how." Chameleons have layers of specialized cells beneath their transparent outer skin. By adjusting the arrangement of these cells, they can control the wavelengths of light that are reflected and absorbed, essentially changing their color in the process.

The speed at which a chameleon changes its color can range from a few seconds to a couple of minutes, depending on the species and situation.

THE REASONS BEHIND THE HUES

So why do chameleons change color? Contrary to popular belief, it's not just for blending into their surroundings. Chameleons also change color for:

COMMUNICATION: Flashy colors might signal excitement or aggression to other chameleons.

TEMPERATURE CONTROL: Light colors can reflect sunlight, while dark colors absorb it, helping them regulate their body temperature.

EMOTIONAL STATE: Yes, chameleons have feelings too! Their colors may change depending on their mood.

The chameleon's emotional "mood ring" is not unique to them; some other reptiles and fish also change color based on their emotional state.

MYTHS VS. FACTS

Alright, let's bust some myths!

MYTH: CHAMELEONS CHANGE COLOR TO MATCH ANY BACKGROUND.

Fact: While they are good at blending in, they can't match complex patterns or unnatural colors.

MYTH: ALL CHAMELEONS CAN DISPLAY A WIDE RANGE OF COLORS.

Fact: Not all species have the same color-changing abilities. Some can only switch between a few shades.

MYTH: CHANGING COLOR IS JUST FOR CAMOUFLAGE.

Fact: As we've learned, camouflage is just one of several reasons chameleons change color.

CHAMELEONS AND HUMANS

Chameleons aren't just creatures that scuttle around trees and shoot out their tongues to snag lunch; they're also legends!

Different cultures around the world have given chameleons all sorts of symbolic meanings. Many people also keep them as pets.

THE LEGEND LIVES ON

African Folklore

In some African stories, chameleons are wise messengers and sometimes even linked to the creation of the world.

Western Symbolism

In Western cultures, the chameleon often represents change or adaptability, thanks to its color-changing abilities.

FUN FACT: In Malawi, the chameleon has a legendary status. According to one myth, it was sent by the gods to deliver the message of eternal life!

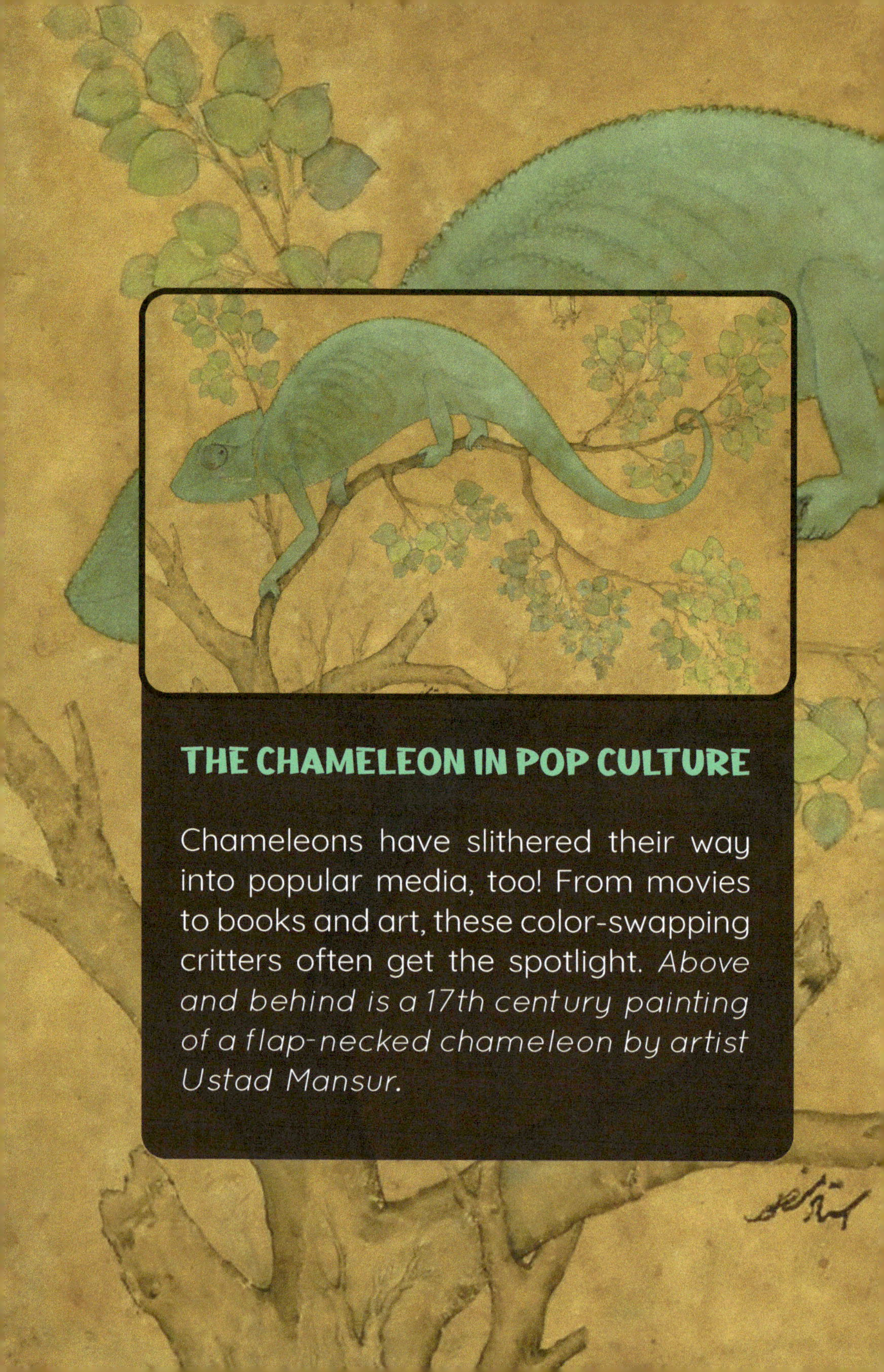

THE CHAMELEON IN POP CULTURE

Chameleons have slithered their way into popular media, too! From movies to books and art, these color-swapping critters often get the spotlight. *Above and behind is a 17th century painting of a flap-necked chameleon by artist Ustad Mansur.*

MOVIES

Remember Pascal, the loyal sidekick in Disney's "**Tangled**"? Yep, he's a chameleon! And have you seen "**Rango**"? This 2011 animated film stars Johnny Depp as the voice of Rango, a chameleon who ends up becoming the sheriff of a Wild West town.

BOOKS

"**The Mixed-Up Chameleon**" by Eric Carle is a popular children's book that explores the theme of identity and individuality.

"**Chameleon, Chameleon**" by Nic Bishop and Joy Cowley is a beautiful picture book that chronicles the journey of a chameleon in the wild as it hunts for food and avoids predators.

CHAMELEONS AS PETS

Are you captivated by chameleons and dreaming of having one as a pet? Well, pump the brakes for a second! Chameleons come in various species, but even the most 'beginner-friendly' ones, like veiled, panther, and Jackson's chameleons, have specific care requirements. Each species has its own set of unique needs that you have to understand inside and out.

THE DO'S AND DON'TS: ADVANCED LEVEL PET CARE

DO: Keep a strict cleaning schedule. A dirty cage can lead to sickness.

DON'T: Think you can play with them like you would a dog or cat. Chameleons mostly prefer to be left alone.

DO: Regularly check temperature and humidity levels. They're sensitive to environmental changes.

DON'T: Expect them to be low-maintenance. Regular vet visits with a reptile specialist are a must.

THEIR HABITAT

Creating a comfortable home for a chameleon is no small feat. You'll need:

A Large Vertical Cage: Chameleons love to climb.

Specialized Lights: A specific UVB light is mandatory for their well-being.

Branches and Plants: For hiding and climbing, but watch out, some plants can be toxic to them!

DINNER TIME

Chameleons are picky eaters. Even the timing of their meals is important; otherwise, they might refuse to eat. The chameleon diet isn't just a matter of dropping some food into a bowl. You'll need live insects, and you'll have to 'dust' them with special vitamin and calcium powders.

REMEMBER!

While chameleons are fascinating, they are definitely not for everyone—especially not for beginners. If you're up for the challenge and ready for some serious pet-care boot camp, then owning a chameleon could be an educational and rewarding experience. But remember, it's a big commitment, so think carefully before you leap—or climb—into the world of chameleon care!

CHAMELEON CONSERVATION
A Reality Check

You've learned a lot about chameleons—their awesome anatomy, tricky tongues, and cool cultural impact. But here's a critical question: How are chameleons doing in the wild? The answer isn't straightforward, but many species are facing challenges due to habitat loss, the pet trade, and climate change.

DID YOU KNOW? Not all chameleon species are endangered. Some are considered 'vulnerable,' which is a step below endangered but still worrisome.

WHAT'S PUTTING CHAMELEONS AT RISK?

CLIMATE CHANGE

Changes in weather patterns can affect the insects chameleons eat and even the plants they live on.

HABITAT LOSS

With forests being cut down and lands being developed, chameleons are losing their homes at an alarming rate.

ILLEGAL PET TRADE

Some people capture wild chameleons to sell as pets, which is harmful to their natural populations.

IT'S NOT ALL BAD NEWS!

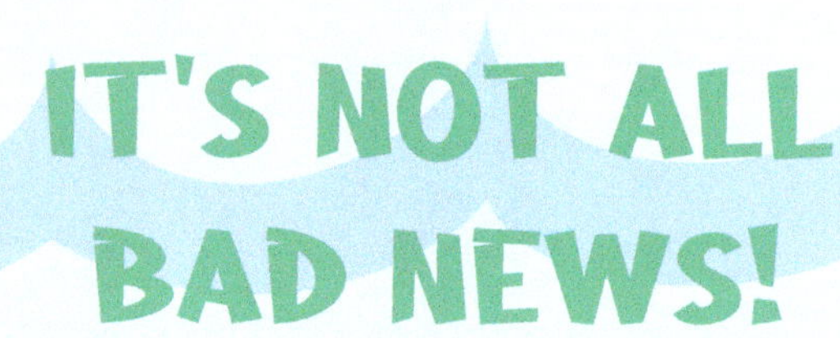

Good news! People are aware of the problems chameleons face and are working to help them.

PROTECTED AREAS: Some countries are creating reserves and national parks where chameleons can live safely.

RESEARCH: Scientists are studying chameleons to better understand their needs and how to protect them.

RESPONSIBLE PET TRADE: Efforts are being made to ensure that pet chameleons are bred in captivity rather than taken from the wild.

MADAGASCAR FAUNA AND FLORA GROUP
Biodiversity Conservation
Chameleon
Specialist Group
THESE ARE JUST A FEW OF THE ORGANIZATIONS THAT WORK HARD TO PROTECT CHAMELEONS AND OTHER WILDLIFE. CHECK OUT THEIR WEBSITES AND SEE HOW YOU CAN GET INVOLVED!
TRAFFIC
the wildlife trade monitoring network
WWF

BECOME A

CHAMELEON HERO

Now that you know how awesome these creatures are and the challenges they face, it's your turn to make a difference. Ready to save the day? Here's how!

SUPPORT CONSERVATION ORGANIZATIONS

You might be thinking, "I'm just a kid; how can I help?" Well, every little bit helps. Consider saving up some of your allowance or hosting a bake sale to raise funds. Then you can donate to charities focused on reptile conservation.

Idea: *Ask for donations to a conservation charity instead of gifts for your next birthday or holiday celebration.*

SYMBOLIC ADOPTION: ADOPT, DON'T SHOP!

Many organizations allow you to "adopt" a chameleon symbolically. You'll get a cute certificate and maybe even a plush chameleon toy, and the funds go toward conservation.

Believe it or not, recycling can also help chameleons. By recycling and reducing waste, you can help combat pollution and climate change—two things that threaten chameleon habitats.

Idea: *Start a recycling program at your school or neighborhood or create a fun energy or water-saving challenge in your household.*

Don't underestimate the power of your voice. Share facts about chameleons and their conservation status with friends and family. The more people know, the more they can help!

Idea: *Create a presentation about chameleons for school or share information on social media.*

Are you ready to leap into action? Remember, you're never too young to make a difference. These fantastic creatures are depending on us, and together, we can help them live long, colorful lives!

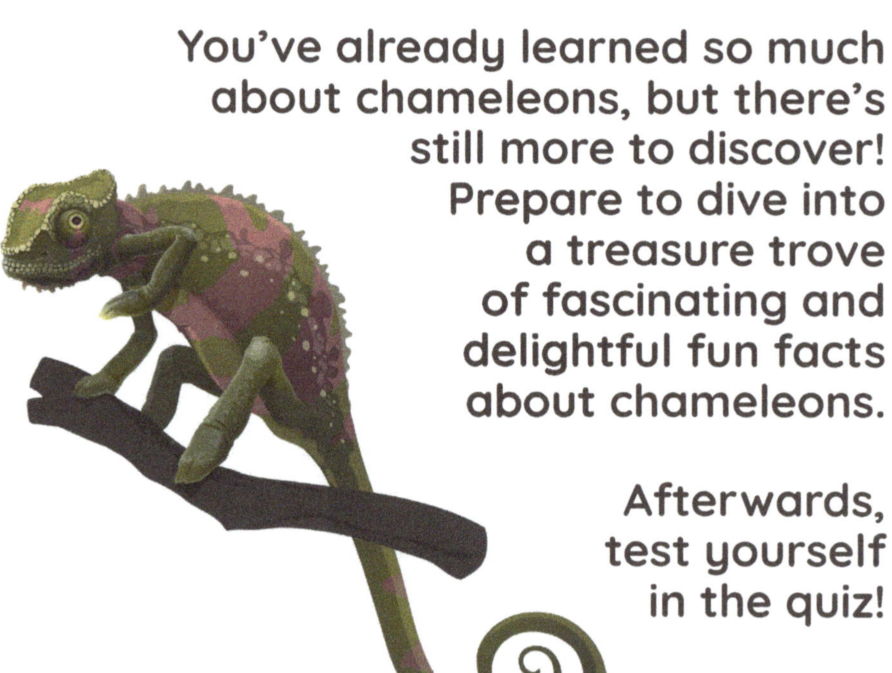

You've already learned so much about chameleons, but there's still more to discover! Prepare to dive into a treasure trove of fascinating and delightful fun facts about chameleons.

Afterwards, test yourself in the quiz!

A chameleon's tongue has a sticky,
mucus-covered tip to help catch prey.

Some chameleons use their tongues
to drink water as well as catch food.

Some species of chameleons can run
surprisingly fast when threatened.

Chameleons have been found at
elevations as high as 15,000 feet!

Only male chameleons tend to
be colorful; females are often
more subdued in hue.

Chameleons sometimes "play dead" to avoid predators.

♥ ♥ ♥

Some chameleons can rotate their eyes to watch two different objects simultaneously.

♥ ♥ ♥

The rosette-like arrangement of scales on a chameleon's skin is unique to each individual, like a fingerprint.

♥ ♥ ♥

Some chameleon species have been observed digging holes (pictured right) to lay their eggs, using their snouts and forelimbs.

© Benny Trapp

THEIR LONG,
STICKY TONGUE
IS A SPECIALIZED
MUSCLE AND NOT AN
EXTENSION OF THE
THROAT.

The veiled chameleon can lay up to
85 eggs at one time.

Some species of chameleons live in
semi-desert conditions and are well-
adapted to the harsh environment.

Chameleons produce a range of
sounds for communication, including
hisses and pops.

Some chameleon species can live
in saltwater mangroves, a unique
adaptation among reptiles.

Chameleons do not have vocal cords; they communicate through body language and color changes.

A chameleon's digestive system is surprisingly efficient, allowing them to go days without eating.

Some chameleons have special cells in their skin that reflect light, giving them a metallic appearance.

Chameleons are excellent climbers but are not very good at walking on flat surfaces.

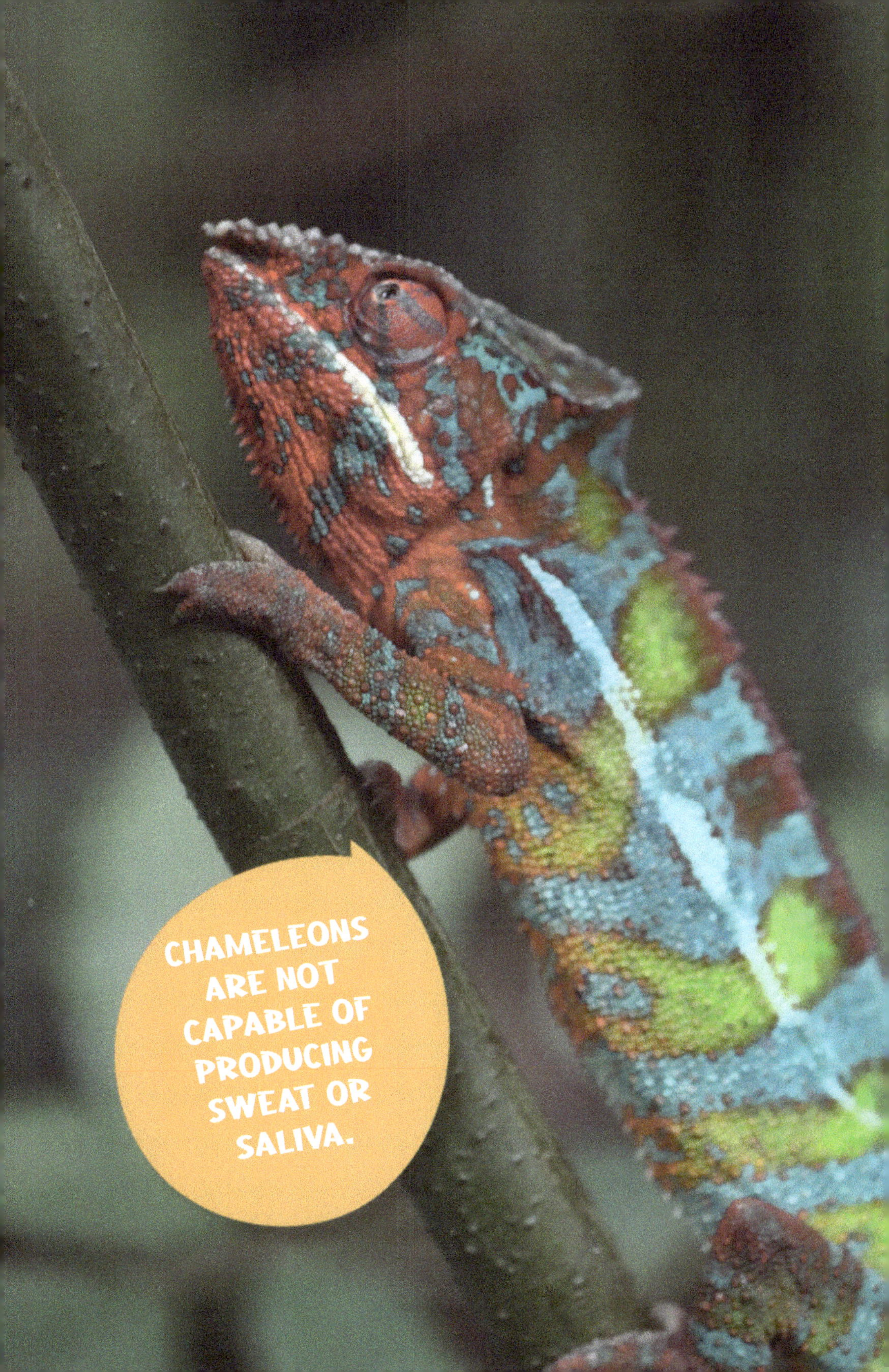
CHAMELEONS
ARE NOT
CAPABLE OF
PRODUCING
SWEAT OR
SALIVA.

CHAMELEON COURTSHIP AND REPRODUCTION

Chameleons have a unique courtship ritual. The males often show off their brightest colors to attract a mate, while females signal their receptiveness or disinterest with their own color changes. Once they mate, most female chameleons lay eggs, burying them in moist soil or sand. These eggs can take anywhere from a few months to over a year to hatch, depending on the species. Some chameleon species give birth to live young, a rarity among reptiles!

Some species have specialized toe
pads that allow them to grip slippery
surfaces.

♥ ♥ ♥

Unlike many other reptiles,
chameleons do not bask in the sun
to regulate their body temperature;
they use their color-changing
abilities instead.

♥ ♥ ♥

Chameleons have a highly
developed sense of balance, aided
by their prehensile tails.

♥ ♥ ♥

Some chameleons have whisker-like
structures on their faces to sense
their environment.

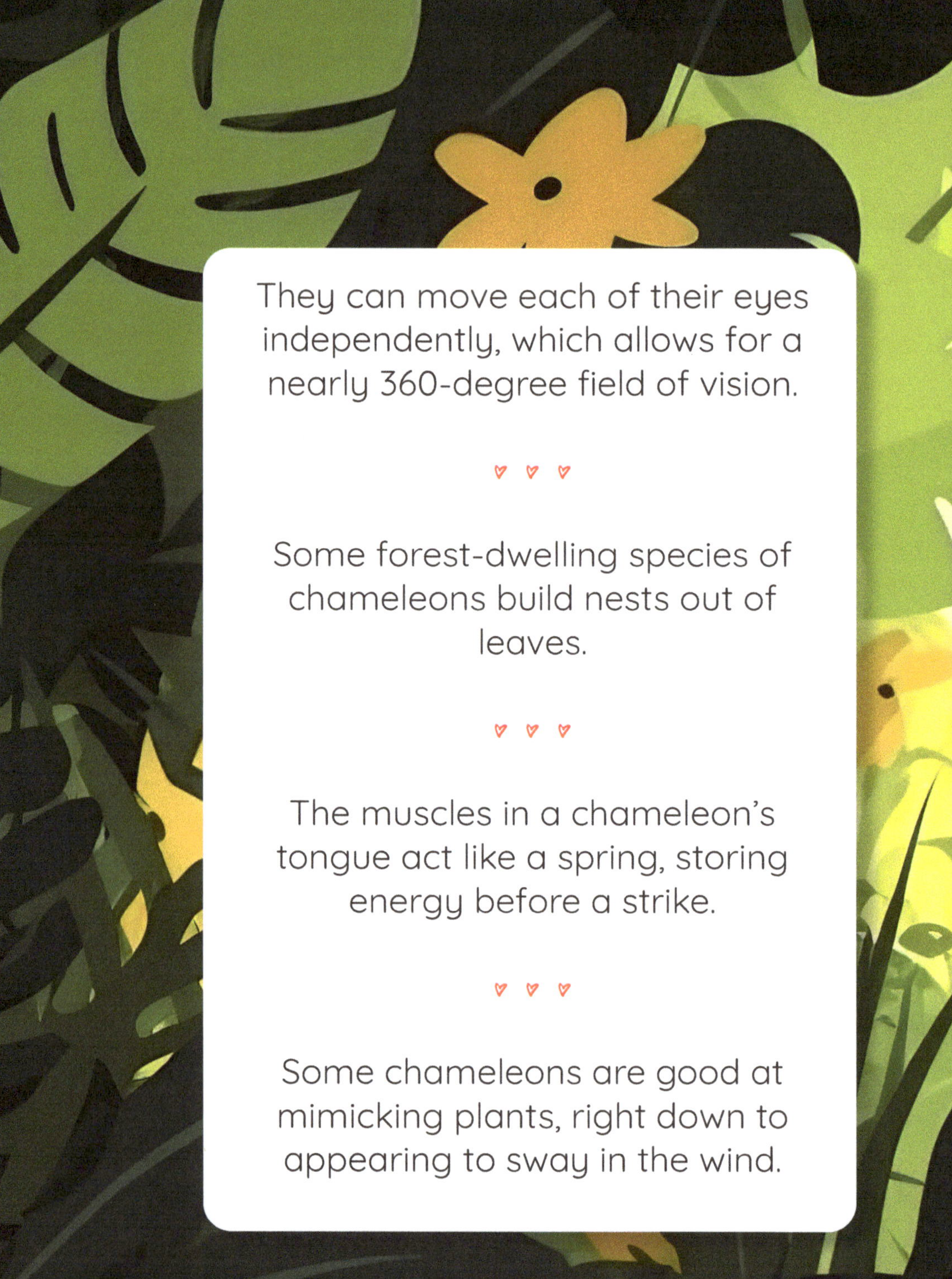

They can move each of their eyes independently, which allows for a nearly 360-degree field of vision.

Some forest-dwelling species of chameleons build nests out of leaves.

The muscles in a chameleon's tongue act like a spring, storing energy before a strike.

Some chameleons are good at mimicking plants, right down to appearing to sway in the wind.

Some chameleon species have been known to live in trees as tall as 30 feet!

Chameleons' bones are very lightweight, aiding in their arboreal lifestyle.

When catching prey, a chameleon's tongue can stretch up to twice its body length.

Chameleons are believed to be among the oldest branches of the iguana suborder.

THEY HAVE SPECIALIZED
" ZYGODACTYLOUS"
FEET-TWO TOES FACING
FORWARD AND TWO
FACING BACKWARD-
TO HELP THEM GRASP
BRANCHES.

Unlike other lizards, chameleons don't
lay eggs in underground burrows;
they often deposit them in leaf litter
or rotting wood.

❤ ❤ ❤

Chameleons sometimes use their
colors to assert territory during
disputes.

❤ ❤ ❤

The rough texture of their skin helps
to break up their outline, making
them harder to see in natural
surroundings.

❤ ❤ ❤

Chameleons have been known to
eat fruit and leaves for additional
vitamins and hydration.

Most chameleons don't live near water, but some species are excellent swimmers.

❧ ❧ ❧

Chameleons can become stressed if they see their own reflection, thinking it's another chameleon.

❧ ❧ ❧

Some chameleons can inflate their bodies to appear bigger and more threatening.

❧ ❧ ❧

A chameleon's skeletal structure is extremely flexible, allowing it to navigate complex terrain easily.

CHAMELEONS
CAN FOCUS
THEIR
EYES
QUICKLY,
ALLOWING
THEM TO
SPOT SMALL
MOVING INSECTS
FROM A DISTANCE.

Chameleon

QUIZ

WERE YOU PAYING ATTENTION?! TEST YOUR NEW CHAMELEON KNOWLEDGE IN OUR QUIZ!

1 What do chameleons primarily use their long, sticky tongues for?

2 Chameleons can move both of their eyes in different directions at the same time. True or false?

3 What's special about a chameleon's feet?

4 What type of chameleon is most commonly kept as a pet?

5 How many species of chameleons are there?

6 Where do chameleons usually lay their eggs?

7 How do chameleons mostly communicate?

8 What do chameleons primarily eat?

9 Which of these is NOT a natural habitat for chameleons: forests, deserts, or polar regions?

10 How can a chameleon's color change help it in the wild?

11 What is the name of the cells that allow chameleons to change color?

ANSWERS

1. Chameleons primarily use their long, sticky tongues for catching prey.
2. True.
3. Chameleon feet are zygodactylous, meaning they have two toes facing forward and two facing backward.
4. The veiled chameleon is most commonly kept as a pet.
5. There are over 160 species of chameleons.
6. Chameleons usually lay their eggs in leaf litter or rotting wood.
7. Chameleons mostly communicate through color changes and body language.
8. Chameleons primarily eat insects.
9. Polar regions are NOT a natural habitat for chameleons.
10. A chameleon's color change can help it in camouflage, thermoregulation, and social interactions.
11. The cells that allow chameleons to change color are called iridophores.
12. Most chameleons are not social animals and prefer solitary lives.

13. Chameleons protect themselves from predators through camouflage and color-changing abilities.
14. Chameleon eyes can move independently, giving them a nearly 360-degree field of vision.
15. Chameleons are adapted to climbing trees with their zygodactylous feet and prehensile tails.
16. A veiled chameleon can lay up to 85 eggs at one time.
17. The chameleon's tail is prehensile and helps in climbing and maintaining balance.
18. Chameleons can make hissing and popping sounds.
19. Chameleons regulate their body temperature by changing their skin color instead of basking in the sun.
20. Some species can swim.
21. Some chameleons can inflate their bodies to look bigger when threatened.
22. Some chameleons use their tongues to drink water. Others lick up raindrops and dew.
23. Some chameleons mimic their environment through their color-changing abilities and sometimes even by swaying like leaves in the wind.

CHAMELEON
WORD SEARCH

D C C X Z B F D S Q S X
R M A D A G A S C A R V
E V C M Z C W S G J U C
P C Q W O X C V V C S X
T T O Q H U D E C Y T Z
I R E L Z X F I X T O R
L E H G O C X L Z R N I
E A V F Z R Q E A W G O
H A B I T A T D C G U T
P J E S A Q S X J D E E
J Z Y G O D A C T Y L F
G S I N S E C T S Z X S

Can you find all the words below in
the word search puzzle on the left?

CAMOUFLAGE   INSECTS   ZYGODACTYL

TONGUE   MADAGASCAR   COLOR

HABITAT   REPTILE   VEILED

SOLUTION

	C										
R	M	A	D	A	G	A	S	C	A	R	
E			M								
P	C			O			V				
T		O			U		E			T	
I			L			F	I			O	
L				O			L			N	
E					R		E	A		G	
H	A	B	I	T	A	T	D		G	U	
										E	
	Z	Y	G	O	D	A	C	T	Y	L	
		I	N	S	E	C	T	S			

SOURCES

"Chameleon". 2023. Britannica Kids. https://kids.britannica.com/kids/article/chameleon/390666.

"Chameleon Facts". 2015. Livescience.Com. https://www.livescience.com/51061-chameleon.html.

Carle, E. (1984). The Mixed-Up Chameleon. New York: HarperCollins.

Frank Glaw, Jörn Köhler, Ted M. Townsend, Miguel Vences - Glaw F, Köhler J, Townsend TM, Vences M (2012) Rivaling the World's Smallest Reptiles: Discovery of Miniaturized and Microendemic New Species of Leaf Chameleons (Brookesia) from Northern Madagascar. PLoS ONE 7(2): e31314. doi:10.1371/journal.pone.0031314

"Getting A Pet Chameleon". 2023. Webmd. https://www.webmd.com/pets/getting-a-pet-chameleon.

"How Do Chameleons Change Colour?". 2023. Encyclopedia Britannica. https://www.britannica.com/story/how-do-chameleons-change-colour.

"How To Care For Pet Veiled Chameleons". 2023. The Spruce Pets. https://www.thesprucepets.com/veiled-chameleon-1238538.

IUCN SSC Chameleon Specialist Group (2021). Conservation Activities. Available at: IUCN Website (Accessed: 5 September 2023).
Jenkins, M. (2001). Chameleons Are Cool. London: Candlewick Press.

Madagascar Fauna and Flora Group (2021). Conservation Work in Madagascar. Available at: Madagascar Fauna and Flora Group Website (Accessed: 5 September 2023).

Necas, P. (2004). Chameleons: Nature's Hidden Jewels. Frankfurt: Edition Chimaira.

"Parson'S Chameleon | Lizard". 2023. Encyclopedia Britannica. https://www.britannica.com/animal/Parsons-chameleon.

Reptile Magazine (2022). Chameleon Care. Available at: Reptile Magazine (Accessed: 5 September 2023).

"Veiled Chameleon (Chamaeleo Calyptratus)". 2023. Inaturalist. https://www.inaturalist.org/taxa/32873-Chamaeleo-calyptratus.

"What You Should Know Before You Get A Chameleon | All Creatures Veterinary Care Center". 2020. All Creatures Veterinary Care Center. https://www.allcreaturesvetcare.com/what-you-should-know-before-you-get-a-chameleon/.

You're Chameleontastic!

As our journey through the world of chameleons comes to an end, we hope you've enjoyed learning about these fascinating animals as much as we enjoyed sharing their story with you.

Your feedback means a lot to us, so we kindly ask you to leave a **review** on the platform where you purchased the book.

Thank you for your support!

ALSO BY JENNY KELLETT

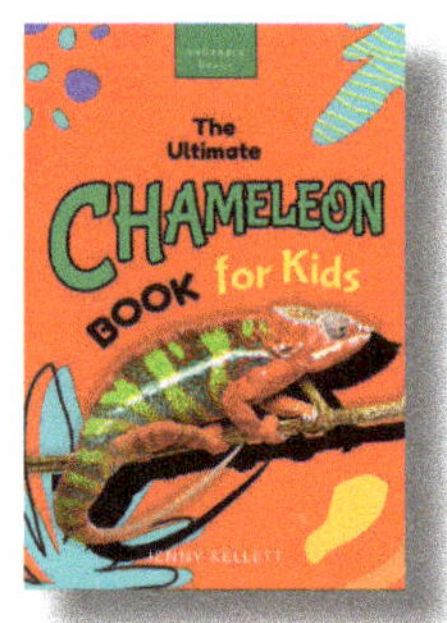

... and more!

Available at

www.bellanovabooks.com

and all major online bookstores.